INVERTEBRATES

THE KINGDOMS OF LIFE

INVERTEBRATES

DR. ALVIN, VIRGINIA, AND ROBERT SILVERSTEIN

TWENTY-FIRST CENTURY BOOKS

A Division of Henry Holt and Company
New York

Twenty-First Century Books
A Division of Henry Holt and Company, Inc.
115 West 18th Street
New York, NY 10011

Henry Holt® and colophon are trademarks of
Henry Holt and Company, Inc.
Publishers since 1866

Published in Canada by Fitzhenry & Whiteside Ltd.
195 Allstate Parkway, Markham, Ontario L3R 4T8

Library of Congress Cataloging-in-Publication Data
Silverstein, Alvin.
Invertebrates / Alvin Silverstein, Virginia Silverstein, and Robert Silverstein. — 1st ed.
p.   cm. — (The Kingdoms of life)
Includes index.
1. Invertebrates—Juvenile literature. I. Silverstein, Virginia B. II. Silverstein, Robert A.
III. Title. IV. Series: Silverstein, Alvin. The Kingdoms of life.
QL362.4.S54 1996   95–45725
592—dc20   CIP
                                                                                                                      AC

ISBN 0-8050-3518-4
First Edition 1996

Designed by Kelly Soong

Printed in the United States of America
All first editions are printed on acid-free paper ∞.
10 9 8 7 6 5 4 3 2 1

Photo credits

Cover photo: William Curtsinger/Photo Researchers, Inc.

p. 6 (clockwise from top right): Dave B. Fleetham/Tom Stack & Associates; Rod Planck/Tom Stack & Associates; Cabisco/Visuals Unlimited; M. I. Walker/Photo Researchers, Inc.; Zig Lezczynski/Earth Scenes; Bill Gause/Photo Researchers, Inc.; p. 7: Dave B. Fleetham/Tom Stack & Associates; p. 8: U.S. Postal Service; p. 10 (left): E. R. Degginger/Animals Animals; pp. 10 (right), 15: David M. Dennis/Tom Stack & Associates; p. 11: Photo Researchers, Inc.; p. 13: Thomas Kitchin/Tom Stack & Associates; p. 13 (inset): Breck P. Kent/Earth Scenes; p. 16 (left): Nancy Sefton/Photo Researchers, Inc.; p. 16 (center): Fred McConnaughey/Photo Researchers, Inc.; p. 16 (right): Larry Lipsky/Tom Stack & Associates; p. 17: Peter Parks/Oxford Scientific Films/Animals Animals; pp. 19, 21 (top), 22: Brian Parker/Tom Stack & Associates; p. 21 (bottom), 33: Oxford Scientific Films/Animal Animals; p. 23: Herb Segars/Animal Animals; p. 24: Mike Bacon/Tom Stack & Associates; p. 25: Breck P. Kent/Animals Animals; p. 28: Denise Tackett/Tom Stack & Associates; p. 31: J. Lotter Gurling/Tom Stack & Associates; p. 32: Patti Murray/Animals Animals; p. 35: Gary Milburn/Tom Stack & Associates; p. 36: Rod Planck/Tom Stack & Associates; p. 38: Randy Morse/Tom Stack & Associates; p. 41: NASA; p. 43: Kathie Atkinson/Animals Animals; pp. 44, 55: Andrew J. Martinez/Photo Researchers, Inc.; p. 47: John Gerlach/Tom Stack & Associates; p. 48: Phil Devries/Oxford Scientific Films/Animals Animals; p. 49: Bruce Davidson/Animals Animals; p. 52: Jeff Foote/Tom Stack & Associates; p. 54: Ashod Frances/Animals Animals; p. 56: Randy Morse/Tom Stack & Associates; p. 57: Alan Baker/Visuals Unlimited.

CONTENTS

The Kingdoms of Life

ANIMALS

Great horned owl

VERTEBRATES

Day octopus

INVERTEBRATES

PLANTS

Silver vase

FUNGI

Hygrophorus mushroom

MONERANS

Cyanobacteria

PROTISTS

Diatoms

INVERTEBRATES

1

OUR LIVING WORLD

CLASSIFICATION MAKES SENSE

Does your family get a lot of junk mail? Sometimes you might be tempted to put all the mail in the recycling bin. But there might be something important, so you have to sort through it. First you might separate the envelopes from the larger items, such as magazines and parcels. The envelopes could be subdivided into a number of categories: letters, bills, checks, and offers of various kinds. Each of these could be further classified—letters that need replies, letters you want to keep, offers you or other family members might find interesting, others that can go straight into the recycling bin. Among the larger items, you'll separate magazines from catalogs. The catalogs you keep can be sorted into categories such as clothing, hobbies, books, music, gardening, or computer supplies. Classifying the mail this way makes it easier to find what you need later, instead of having to sort through the whole messy pile each time.

Large machines help sort the mail at a U.S. post office.

Classifying makes sense whenever you have to deal with a lot of very varied things—and it would be hard to think of any collection of things more numerous and varied than the living organisms in our world. You may not think very often about the variety of animals, plants, and other creatures who share your world, but knowledge of how they are related can be very useful.

What if, for example, you were an alien explorer from another planet, who had just landed on earth? You'd want to find out as much as you could about our living creatures, as quickly as possible. Which ones might be dangerous? Which might be helpful? Which might be good to eat? You'd find so many different kinds of creatures, how could you possibly make sense of them all? You might begin by taking careful notes on your pocket recorder, describing the characteristics of each creature you saw—how large it was, whether it moved, made noises, seemed to respond to what you did, and whether there was just one of its kind, a few, or many. After a while you'd have enough information to begin sorting the life-forms you met into categories, to classify them.

So far we have not explored any other planets, nor have any alien explorers visited us. But dealing with our own planet has presented challenges just as great and exciting. People have been studying and sorting out earth's living creatures ever since the first humans worried about catching enough animals and gathering enough plants to eat.

CLASSIFICATION: A SORTING OF SORTS

Classification is the process of dividing objects into related groups. **Taxonomy** is the science of classifying or arranging living things into groups based on characteristics they share. It comes from the Greek words *taxis*, which means "arrangement," and *nomos*, which means "law."

Alien explorers would distinguish fairly quickly between nonliving things, such as rocks and water, and living things that can grow, change, and respond to their surroundings. But they might group the living things into some categories that would seem strange to us.

For thousands of years humans divided living things into two main groups: plants (organisms that make their own food, are usually green, and do not move around on their own) and animals (more active organisms that may move about, perceive and react to their surroundings, and need to eat to get nourishment for their growth and activities). Today most scientists divide living things into five kingdoms of life.

Each **kingdom** can be subdivided into smaller groups, called **phyla (phylum** is

An ant and a spider belong to the same large phylum, Arthropoda, but an ant (left) has six legs and is further classified as an insect. A spider (right) has eight legs, so it is an arachnid.

singular), whose members have more characteristics in common with one another than with other living things. An ant and a spider, for example, have many differences. (An ant has three main body parts and six legs; a spider has two main body parts and eight legs.) Yet they resemble each other much more than they resemble jellyfish, clams, or tigers. Both ants and spiders belong to the same large phylum—Arthropoda—in the animal kingdom, but within the phylum of arthropods they belong to different **classes**: ants are insects, and spiders are arachnids. Classes are further divided into **orders**, orders into **families**, families into **genera** (**genus** is singular), and genera into **species**.

Every living thing has a specific place in our modern classification system. Its place shows how closely it is related to other living things. You can tell a living thing's place by its

MEMORY AIDS

Silly sentences can help you remember lists. The first letters of

King **P**hilip **C**atches **O**ld **F**ish, **G**ets **S**ick

can help you remember the major groups of the scientific classification system:

Kingdom, **P**hylum, **C**lass, **O**rder, **F**amily, **G**enus, **S**pecies.

scientific name: this is its genus and species. These names are usually made from Latin and Greek words, such as *Formica rufa* (the red ant) and *Latrodectus mactans* (the black widow spider).

LINNAEUS STARTED IT ALL

Our modern classification system was devised by an eighteenth-century Swedish botanist and naturalist, Carl Linnaeus. His system is called **binomial nomenclature** (which means "two-name naming") because he gave each kind of organism a genus and species name. Linnaeus also grouped living organisms according to their structure, setting up a framework that showed the relationships among all the forms of life on our planet.

Carl Linnaeus (1707–1778) devised the scientific method of naming living things. He wrote books in Latin on the classification of plants and animals.

2

THE ANIMAL KINGDOM

If you were an alien explorer looking for earth creatures to communicate with, you'd undoubtedly take the closest look at those most like you—perhaps not physically, but in certain key abilities. They would be able to see or hear or find out what was going on, and they would respond to this information in various active ways. Most of the creatures that could do this would turn out to belong to just one of the major kingdoms of life: the animals.

WHAT IS AN ANIMAL?

Animals are organisms whose bodies are made up of many microscopic cells that work together, each doing its own job. Animals do not make their own food and must obtain nourishment from other organisms. Most animals digest their food inside a cavity in their bodies. Most move from place to place.

WHERE DID THE FIRST ANIMAL COME FROM?

Scientists believe that animals, like plants, arose from single-celled creatures—**protists**. Some of these single cells began living together, sharing food and shelter. Eventually some members of the cell community became specialized for particular jobs, such as getting food or producing stingers to defend the group against enemies. Then they were no longer members of a cell community but parts of a single organism.

No one is sure which protists are most like the ones that gave rise to animals. Actually, multicelled animals may have arisen several separate times. The earliest animal fossils show a type of animal that arose about 670 million years ago and lived for about

The Burgess Shale (left) in western Canada is famous for its fossils, including those of trilobites (right). Trilobites were early flat shellfish that crawled along the sea floor.

100 million years before it died out. It was not like the animals alive today. Nearly all modern animals have a body that is basically a tube with a tube-shaped cavity inside it. But these early animals had no tubular internal structure. Most were flat like leaves. Some were quilted like a mattress.

Between 590 million and 505 million years ago, simple animals with an inner cavity arose. These early organisms did survive and became the ancestors of all the animals living today.

ONWARD AND UPWARD

Scientists have already named and classified more than a million different kinds of animals. Nobody knows how many more there are, hidden in dense rain forests or in the depths of the seas. Each year hundreds of new animals are discovered, studied, and carefully fitted into the scheme of life. Today animals are classified into about thirty phyla, depending on various characteristics, including the following:

1. the basic body plan
2. the number of layers of tissues (groups of cells working together)
3. the way body parts are arranged
4. the way an organism develops into an adult animal

Another common grouping distinguishes between **vertebrates** (animals with backbones) and **invertebrates** (animals without backbones). The invertebrates, the animals that will be the focus of this book, include about 95 percent of the animals living today—all except for eight classes in the phylum Chordata.

The way our modern classification system is arranged shows how living things evolved from simple organisms to more and more complex ones. This is especially clear as we move from phylum to phylum in the animal kingdom. The animals in each phylum have specific evolutionary advances that the members of the previous phyla do not share.

The major invertebrate phyla of the animal kingdom are

Porifera (sponges)

Cnidaria (hydra, corals, sea anemones, jellyfish)

Ctenophora (comb jellies)

Platyhelminthes (flatworms, flukes, tapeworms)

Nemertea (ribbon worms)

Rotifera (rotifers)

Nematoda (roundworms)

Annelida (segmented worms: earthworms, polychaetes, leeches)

Tardigrada (water bears)

Mollusca (mollusks: monoplacophores, chitons, snails, slugs, clams, oysters, nautiluses, octopuses, squids)

Arthropoda (horseshoe crabs, ticks, mites, scorpions, spiders, water fleas, copepods, barnacles, lobsters, shrimp, millipedes, centipedes, insects)

Echinodermata (sea stars, sand dollars, sea urchins, sea cucumbers)

This is a fossil of a horseshoe crab (Mesolimulus sp.) *that lived during the Jurassic period, 205 to 138 million years ago. It looks very much like a modern horseshoe crab.*

TREASURE HUNTING

What would you do if you found a shoe box full of old baseball cards up in your grandparents' attic? The first thing you'd want to do would be to sort through the cards to see which ones were there. But looking through the many cards would soon get confusing unless you had some kind of plan. Perhaps you might try to put them in alphabetical order, according to the players' last names. That could be a good way for checking them against a catalog list to find out how much each card would be worth to serious collectors.

But you could also sort them according to the year each card was printed or group them by teams. You might want to divide the cards into categories according to each player's position: pitcher, catcher, infielder, and outfielder. Each group could be subdivided in various ways: outfielders into right, left, and center fielders; or pitchers who won Cy Young Awards, or played in the World Series, or won more than twenty games in a season. Each sorting would provide information and help you to compare the players' records.

3

AT THE BOTTOM OF
THE ANIMAL KINGDOM

The sponges that you may use for wiping up in the kitchen or bathroom are probably made of plastic. But you may have a bath sponge that is the "real thing." Although it is just as lifeless as a plastic sponge, it is the dried skeleton of an animal that was once alive.

Early naturalists thought sponges were plants—a logical idea since they don't move and do look rather like plants. But in the mid-eighteenth century it was decided to regard them as "zoophytes," or plant-animals. Today, most scientists consider the 10,000 or so species of sponges the simplest animals and classify them in the phylum **Porifera**. They believe sponges may have evolved, about 600 million years ago, from a different ancestor than other members of the animal kingdom. In fact, some taxonomists place them in their own subkingdom, **Parazoa**, which means "beside the animals."

A variety of sponges: Red vase sponge (left) from the Caribbean, blue tube sponge (center) from the Philippines, and sponges (right) from the Florida Keys.

LIVING FILTERS

Sponges can be found in all of the seas of the world, and some are found in freshwater lakes, ponds, and rivers. They start out as tiny swimming **larvae** (immature forms) but soon settle down to spend the rest of their lives attached to rocks, shells, or other surfaces. Sponges come in many shapes (fans, vases, cups, funnels, trumpets, or tubes) and range from 1 inch to nearly 3 feet (2.5 centimeters to 0.9 meter) high or wide. Many live in colonies.

In single-celled organisms, one cell must take care of all the things that are necessary to keep it alive. But the cells that make up sponges perform different tasks. Some cells give the organism its shape, some help feed it, and some reproduce it. But sponges don't have tissues or organs. Their bodies are made up of two layers of cells, separated by a clear jelly.

Porifera means "pore bearer." The outside of a sponge's body is filled with pores that work like the holes in a strainer. Water enters through the pores. Some of the pores strain out food; others let wastes out. The cells on the inner body wall have whiplike flagella that lash back and forth, moving water containing oxygen toward the cells and carrying waste products such as carbon dioxide away from the cells. But there is no real coordination between the different cells that make up a sponge—it is more like separate individuals joined together into one animal.

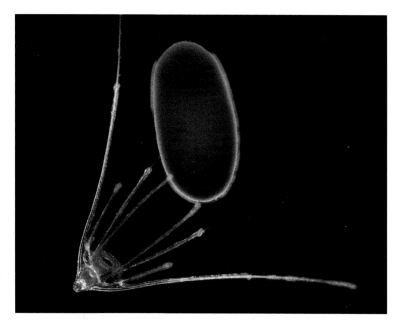

The reddish oval in this picture is the free-swimming larva, called a planula, of a sponge.

THIS IS A HOLDUP!

Most sponges have a skeleton of minerals or protein fibers in their jelly layer to provide protection and support. In some this skeleton is made of tiny needles or other shapes (**spicules**) that are as hard as stone. In others the skeleton is soft and elastic. Venus's-flower-baskets are sponges whose skeletons look like spun glass. Scientists use the shape and composition of spicules to classify different species of sponges. The skeleton is removed when sponges are cleaned and dried for use by people.

Sponge farmers cut up living sponges into pieces and place each piece on a rock or concrete block underwater. A few years later each piece has become a full-sized sponge. Some sponges actually reproduce in a similar way: a part of the sponge's body breaks off and grows into a new sponge. But most sponges produce **egg** and **sperm** cells. The sperm are released into the water and are pulled into other sponges. There

A "REPUBLIC OF CELLS"

If you cut up a living sponge into small pieces and press each piece through a nylon stocking into a jar filled with water, you will wind up with individual sponge cells floating around. But as the days go by, the single cells gather together. Eventually they form a perfect miniature sponge, the same shape as the large one you originally cut up. The individual cells carry the genetic instructions for making a whole sponge of their species. And they can regroup to re-form the sponge's simple body structure.

THE SPONGE THAT ATE TAXONOMY

Taxonomists define the phylum Porifera on the basis of the typical system for filtering water through the sponge's body. But in 1995 French scientists discovered a new sponge species that turned the old definition upside down. In the deep, still waters of the Mediterranean Sea where the new species was found, there is very little food. A sponge that just quietly filtered out organic matter would probably starve to death. But the new sponge, which lives in caves, is a carnivore! Threadlike filaments extending from the sponge's body are covered with tiny hook-shaped structures that grab onto small swimming creatures and stick like Velcro. Then filaments grow over the sponge's prey and digest it.

A sponge crab (Dromidiopsis dormia) *carries pieces of sponge on its back to use as camouflage.*

they join with egg cells to form larvae. The tiny larvae swim about for a few days, then find a new spot and settle down for life.

Most animals don't consider sponges good to eat, but many small fish, crabs, and shrimp make their homes inside sponges. The sponge crab uses sponges as camouflage. It tears off a piece of sponge and attaches it to its shell. The sponge grows on the crab's back, and other animals think the crab is a sponge and leave it alone.

4

~~~~~~

THE NEXT STEP UP

~~~~~~

A pretty piece of coral that you buy in a store and a dried up jellyfish that you see washed up on the beach might not look like they have anything in common, but they belong to the same phylum, **Cnidaria**. Jellyfish, sea anemones, corals, and the hydra are all cnidarians.

GUT FEELINGS

Cnidarians' general body plan might seem somewhat similar to that of sponges, but they are actually more complex. An old name for their phylum, Coelenterata, means "hollow gut"—a major advance in evolution. Inside a cnidarian is a hollow, baglike **gastrovascular cavity** with a single opening at one end, through which food and water enter and wastes leave. (*Gastro* means "digestive" and *vascular* refers to circulating body fluids.) Food is partially digested within this cavity, and the cells lining it absorb food chemicals and oxygen from the water. (The lining cells are epithelial cells, like the cells that line your mouth and digestive system.)

Unlike sponges, cnidarians have simple body tissues, such as nervous tissue. (The nerve cells that help to coordinate the work of the various body cells are linked together in a net, so if you touch one part of a cnidarian, its whole body reacts.) A cnidarian's body is made up of two layers of cells, like the bread in a sandwich, with jellylike material between them, and it has **radial symmetry**, with no distinct right and left sides.

A cnidarian's mouth is surrounded by tentacles. These tentacles are equipped with stinging cells called **cnidoblasts**. (Animals with a similar body plan but without stinging cells are classified in a separate phylum, **Ctenophora**.)

There are two main forms of cnidarians: the **polyp** ("many feet") and the **medusa**

Sea anemones, such as this club-tipped anemone (Corynactis californica), often look like flowers. They belong to class Anthozoa.

(from the monster in Greek mythology who had snakes for hair). The polyp is shaped like a vase and is attached to a rock or shell. The medusa has an umbrella-shaped body, like an upside-down polyp, and is free-swimming. Some cnidarians go through both forms at different stages. There are about 10,000 species of cnidarians, grouped into three classes: **Hydrozoa** (such as the hydra—a polyp); **Scyphozoa** (jellyfish—medusas), and **Anthozoa** (sea anemones and corals—polyps).

MINIATURE MONSTERS

The hydra is the simplest cnidarian. It is an animal measuring 0.5 inch (1.3 centimeters) that lives in ponds. It looks like a piece of frayed string, but under a microscope you can see that each strand is really a tentacle. In Greek mythology Hercules battled the Hydra, a many-headed monster. When he cut off one of its heads, it grew two new ones. Much like the mythological monster it was named after, if a hydra is cut into pieces, each one will grow into a new animal. Hydras can bend because of musclelike cells. They move by turning somersaults on their tentacles.

This tiny hydra is in the process of reproducing by budding. Small hydras grow from the parent's body, then break off after they are fully developed.

BEAUTIFUL, BUT BEWARE . . .

The hydra has only a polyp stage, and it lives alone, but most other hydrozoans have both polyp and medusa stages and are colonial. The Portuguese man-of-war looks like a jellyfish but is actually a **colony** of medusas and polyps living together. The pink or blue gas-filled float that sits on top of the water is one animal. The other animals in the colony live under the float. Some of the animals use their long tentacles to capture food. Other members of the colony eat and digest the food, then share it with the rest of the colony. Still other members make the sperm and eggs to reproduce the colony. The tentacles may reach out 60 feet (18 meters). At the tips are stingers that can paralyze large fish and even seriously injure humans.

JELLYFISH

Jellyfish belong to the class Scyphozoa ("cup animals"). They are one of the oldest animals and have changed very little since they first appeared at least 600 million years ago. Today there are about 200 kinds. If you see a large jellyfish while swimming in the ocean, it is probably a moon jellyfish. This practically colorless jellyfish grows up to 2 feet (61 centimeters) wide and can be found in every ocean.

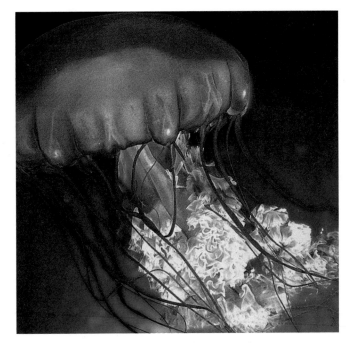

A sea nettle jellyfish (Chrysaora fuscescens)

Some jellyfish are tiny, just the size of your fingertip. But the tentacles of the pink jellyfish of the North Atlantic can be up to 200 feet (61 meters) long! A jellyfish's body is mostly water. If it is washed up on shore, it will dry up and practically disappear, leaving only a circle of film.

Male jellyfish produce sperm cells, and females produce egg cells. Sperm and egg join to form a tiny larva that swims around for a while before attaching to the bottom of the sea. It grows as a polyp for several months, then forms buds that break off and swim away to become medusas.

FLOWER ANIMALS

Jellyfish swim freely through the water, but the members of the class Anthozoa ("flower animals")—such as sea anemones, sea fans, and sea pens—spend their lives attached to rocks or shells or the mud at the bottom of the ocean. Some live alone, but some, such as corals, live in colonies.

Most corals are very small. Their bodies produce a limy substance around them that hardens into a chalky cup. This outer "skeleton" protects the soft body inside. During the day the corals hide inside their protective shell, but at night they stretch out their tentacles like flowers to catch small animals swimming by.

As a coral colony grows larger, it creates its own special shape. Some are branched like trees, but others are flat like boards. Many islands in the Pacific were formed by corals. When these animals die, their skeletons remain behind and new corals attach on top of the old skeletons. Over hundreds of thousands of years corals have built up huge reefs filled with caves and ledges. The largest coral reef in the world is the Great Barrier Reef, off the eastern coast of Queensland, Australia. It is 95 miles (153 kilometers) wide and more than 1,250 miles (2,012 kilometers) long! This is the largest structure ever built by living organisms. Many kinds of sea creatures make their homes in coral reefs.

COMB JELLIES

Scientists classify the ninety species of comb jellies (also called sea walnuts or cat's eyes) in their own phylum, Ctenophora ("comb bearers"). The name comes from eight rows of "combs" (bands of hairlike cilia joined together) that are used for swimming. These combs may glow with a greenish or bluish light in the dark. Comb jellies' tentacles do not contain stinging cells. Instead they have sticky cells to catch prey.

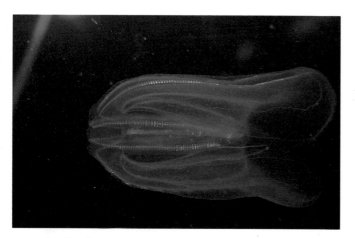

A comb jelly glowing in the dark

5

WORMS, WORMS, AND MORE WORMS

When you hear the word *worm*, you probably picture an earthworm, or the "worm" in an apple. Early taxonomists grouped all the long, thin, squiggly animals into one phylum: Vermes (Latin for "worm"). Today, scientists know that many of the wormlike creatures of the world are very different from one another. After cnidarians on the evolutionary ladder come several phyla of worms, including flatworms; roundworms; and true, or segmented, worms.

FLATWORMS

Flatworms, as their name suggests, are flat like ribbons. The name of their phylum, **Platyhelminthes**, means "flat worms." They may not look as complex as a Portuguese man-of-war, but actually they represent a major step up on the evolutionary ladder. Flatworms are the first animals to have **bilateral symmetry**. This means that if you drew a line down the center of a flatworm's body, the two halves would look like mirror images of each other. Flatworms are also the first with separate "head" and "tail" ends, with nerve cells and sense organs clustered in the head end. Their bodies have three separate layers of cells, rather than two. They are the first animals with different types of tissues grouped into organs to perform various body functions.

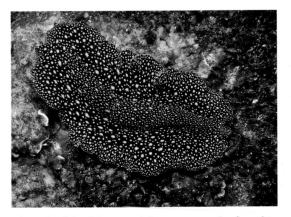

The colorful gold-spotted flatworm can be found in the Galápagos Islands.

Scientists are not sure whether flatworms evolved from cnidarians or developed independently from protist ancestors. But most believe that the rest of the bilaterally symmetrical animals may have evolved from animals resembling free-living flatworms. About 30,000 species of flatworms are known. Taxonomists divide them into three classes: **Turbellaria** (the free-living flatworms), **Trematoda** (flukes), and **Cestoda** (tapeworms).

Planarians are flatworms that are often examined in science classes. These worms, about 1 inch (2.5 centimeters) long, are found in ponds and springs. They have arrow-shaped heads and pointed tails. Like the hydra, planarians have a cavity that is used for digestion and circulation with a single opening for eating and getting rid of wastes. (The mouth is in the middle of the worm.) Planarians also have several simple organs: two eye spots in the head end, reproductive organs, simple kidneys, and a muscular throat (pharynx). Muscle cells help these animals to move. Planarians have a simple nervous system, too, with a tiny "brain" in the head and nerves running down to the tail end.

Flukes are parasites that live inside other animals. A fluke's small, oval body looks like a deflated balloon. It has an armorlike coat around it called a cuticle, to protect itself from its host's digestive juices. It holds on with suckers and sucks tissue and body fluids into its digestive tract. Each fluke is both a male and a female, and most of its body is filled with reproductive organs.

Flukes can have complicated life cycles, passing through one or two different hosts before they get to the final host, where they reproduce. Blood flukes (genus *Schistosoma*), for example, first live in snails before they enter their final hosts—humans.

Tapeworms are long and flat like ribbons. They can get into the intestines of many animals, including cats, dogs, and humans. At the tapeworm's head end are suckers and a circle of hooks that it uses to attach to the intestinal wall of its victim. A tapeworm doesn't have a mouth or digestive system. Through its skin it absorbs already-digested food materials from its victim's intestines. The tapeworm's body is just a series of baglike segments that are filled with reproductive

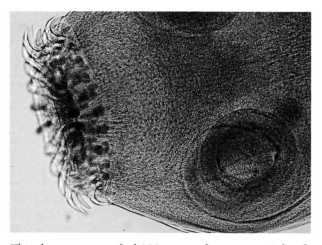

This close-up, magnified 100 times, of a tapeworm's head shows the hooks it uses to attach to the intestinal wall of its victim.

organs of both sexes. When a segment is filled with eggs, it breaks off and passes out of its host's body in the feces. A full-grown beef tapeworm can be 80 feet (24 meters) long!

RIBBON WORMS

There are about 650 species of ribbon worms, belonging to phylum **Nemertea**. Some of these marine worms can grow to 90 feet (27 meters) long. Ribbon worms are of interest to biologists who are trying to reconstruct the path of evolution. Ribbon worms are closely related to flatworms, but they have some important advances. One is a "one-way" digestive system, which begins with a mouth and ends in an anus. Cnidarians and flatworms, with only one opening, cannot eat and get rid of wastes simultaneously. With a one-way digestive system, animals can eat continuously, and different parts of the digestive system can become more specialized.

ROUNDWORMS

The roundworms of phylum **Nematoda** came up with the next major evolutionary advance: a sealed, fluid-filled tube or body cavity. This provides some skeletal support, allowing these animals to move much better. Scientists are not sure how many species of roundworms there are; estimates range up to 500,000. Roundworms are found just about everywhere—in the soil; in lakes, ponds, and oceans; and even in drinking water. (There may be 100,000 in a single handful of dirt.) Most roundworms are harmless, but some are parasites on plants and animals. About fifty kinds are parasites in people and are a major cause of death and illness around the world. More than a billion people are infected by roundworms.

Nematoda means "threadlike," and free-living roundworms look like tiny pieces of

EVOLUTION CAN GO BACKWARD

We usually think of evolution as a development from simpler to more complex forms. Yet scientists believe that tapeworms evolved from free-living ancestors similar to planarians. In adapting to life as a parasite, their bodies became simpler but more *efficient*: they lost the organs they no longer needed.

thread. But some of the parasites can be up to 3 feet (nearly 1 meter) long. Round-worms have a digestive system with a mouth at one end and an anus at the other. They also have a separate circulatory system, made up of muscular tubes. Roundworms were the first in the animal kingdom to have blood cells.

TRUE WORMS

The 9,000 or so species of true worms belong to the phylum **Annelida** (which means "little rings"). An annelid's body is made up of segments or rings. This is an advance in evolution, because each segment is a unit of the body, like the cars in a train, allowing for specialization of different body parts. Bristles on the outside of each segment are used for feeding, swimming, or breathing. Annelids are divided into three classes according to the amount of bristles the worms have. Class **Polychaeta** ("many bristles") includes the bristle worms; **Oligochaeta** ("a few bristles") includes the earthworms; and **Hirudinea** includes leeches, which have no bristles.

True worms have much more complicated bodies than other worms. Their digestive system contains several organs, such as a muscular pharynx, a gullet, a double stomach (which includes a crop for storing food and a muscular gizzard to grind up the food), an intestine, and a rectum. The circulatory system contains two long blood vessels that branch off to the segments to circulate the blood, as well as pairs of muscular tubes that serve as simple hearts. Two sets of muscles help the earthworm to wriggle along, burrowing through the ground. Its nervous system is also much more developed, with a distinct "brain" in the head end.

Annelids and all of the living things that evolved later have an internal body cavity called a **coelom**. (Unlike the body cavity that first appeared in roundworms, the coelom is fully lined with musclelike cells.) The coelom is a major evolutionary advance. Not only does it provide support, but it allows the organs to be suspended inside. This development allowed later animals to develop complex organs such as the expanding and contracting lung and the long coiled intestine.

Earthworms are good for gardens because they break up the soil so that air and water can get to plant roots. They don't just tunnel through soil—they eat it! The soil passes through the earthworm's digestive system and food matter is removed.

There are about 3,000 species of earthworms. Common earthworms (*Lumbricus terrestris*) are also called night crawlers because they come up to the surface at night to feed on fallen leaves or to mate. (Each earthworm is both male and female, although it must mate with another earthworm; then both worms lay eggs.) They grow to about 1 foot (30 centimeters) long, but the giant earthworms in Australian rain forests (*Megascolides australis*) may be 12 feet (3.6 meters) long and stretch to 21 feet (6 meters)!

Most of the other 12,000 or so species of annelids are bristle worms. They include ragworms (which have a jagged look because of the paddles that stick out from their segments) and bloodworms (named for their red color). Some bristle worms have distinct head, trunk, and tail regions. Most have tentacles, which may be covered with bristles. Many have tiny eyes, sharp jaws, and a pair of muscular bulges on each body segment that act like feet and breathing organs. Some have bristles or paddlelike structures on each "foot" to help them swim through the water or wriggle through sand.

Most bristle worms live in the ocean inside tubes that they build out of a limy substance, or by mixing mucus with sand. Feather-duster worms have feathery tentacles that they use to capture food. They quickly hide inside their tubes when danger is near. Trumpet worms make U-shaped tunnels in the sand and bury themselves upside down. They pull water into the tunnel, bringing in oxygen and food.

Polychaeta **tube worms** can thrive at great depths in the ocean, especially near hydrothermal vents. The water there, heated up in crevices in the earth's crust, has high concentrations of minerals and sulfide compounds, which provide food and energy sources for a whole chain of life. In the early 1990s, researchers in the undersea exploring vessel *Alvin* observed an area of the sea bottom about 1.5 miles (2.4 kilometers) deep, where lava had flowed out and killed the undersea life. Within two years, there was a thriving new animal community, including tube worms 4 feet (more than 1 meter) long.

A maroon feather-duster worm from the South China Sea

Leeches are parasites that have suckers at both ends. With fewer segments than other annelids (a total of thirty-three segments), no bristles, and less-developed sense organs, they are streamlined for their highly specialized life. Leeches suck blood. (A leech can drink ten times its own weight in blood at a single meal!) A special chemical in their saliva, hirudin, prevents the hosts' blood from clotting so that leeches can keep feeding from their victims. In the past, doctors used leeches to suck out the "bad blood" of their patients, a treatment that was supposed to cure numerous ailments. That is why the leech's scientific name is *Hirudo medicinalis*. Recently doctors have started using leeches again to reduce swelling and promote healing after certain kinds of surgery.

MAKE YOUR OWN EARTHWORM FARM

If you carefully dig up a foot or two of garden soil, you will probably find some earthworms. You can observe how they live and how they change the soil by placing them in a homemade earthworm farm. Fill a large glass jar about two-thirds of the way to the top with alternating layers of sand, soil, and dead leaves, and place the earthworms on the top layer. Wrap the jar in a dark cloth or paper bag and keep it in a cool, dark place. Water the soil a little every two or three days to keep it damp but not soggy. (Earthworms breathe through their moist skin, but they could drown if you put in too much water.)

In a few days you will see some of the earthworms' tunnels through the soil. (If you don't keep the jar dark most of the time, the worms will make all their tunnels in the inner part of the soil, where you can't see them. Strong light can injure or even kill earthworms, and they avoid it. They do not have eyes, but they can sense light with special cells in their skin.) Place some fresh leaves on top of the soil and observe when and how the worms feed. What happens to the different-colored layers of sand and soil?

6

SOFT-BODIED "SHELLFISH"

Every day millions of shells wash up on the beaches of the world. These shells belonged to soft-bodied animals called mollusks. The name of their phylum, **Mollusca**, means "soft"—a bit ironic, considering that most of them are best known for their hard shells. Mollusca is the second-largest animal phylum, with about 100,000 living species. They include many familiar sea creatures such as clams, octopuses, squids, and oysters, as well as the familiar land-dwelling snails and slugs.

IS THERE A "TYPICAL" MOLLUSK?

Clams, octopuses, and snails might not seem to have much in common, but they all share several typical mollusk traits. Mollusks have a large, muscular foot that is used for creeping along rocks and as an anchor. They have a covering of tissue over their internal organs, called a **mantle** (cloak), which in most species secretes a hard limy shell over their soft bodies. The shell offers protection against predators. Their digestive system is made up of a mouth, throat, gullet, stomach, intestine, and anus. And many species have a **radula**, a tonguelike organ with rows of horny "teeth," used to rasp off bits of food.

Water-dwelling mollusks use gills to get their oxygen from water. Land-dwelling mollusks use lungs to get their oxygen from the air. A simple heart pumps blood through branched blood vessels. The nervous system is made of two pairs of nerve cords. One goes to the foot and the other to the mantle. Some mollusks have eyes and other sense organs.

Some scientists believe that mollusks and annelids arose from the same ancestor. Most mollusks and marine annelids pass through the same type of larval form in their development. But unlike the annelids, mollusks do not have segmented bodies.

LIVING FOSSILS

The most primitive mollusks belong to the class **Monoplacophora**. They have simple digestive tracts and thin, round shells. Until the 1950s, scientists had seen only fossils from this class. Then some living specimens (*Neopilina galatheae*) were discovered 2 miles (3.2 kilometers) down on the ocean floor off Costa Rica. Now at least eight species are known.

STAY-AT-HOMES

Class **Polyplacophora** includes about 600 species of chitons (sometimes called sea cradles). They have flattened oval bodies, with shells divided into seven or eight overlapping plates. (The name of the class means "carrying many plates.") Some are smaller than your thumb, but giant chitons may be more than 1 foot (30 centimeters) long. Most of the time a chiton stays in one spot; its flat foot acts like a suction cup. If it ever leaves its home, it always comes back to the exact same spot. In fact, some chitons live their whole lives in depressions formed by generation after generation of ancestors that lived in the same place.

The lined chiton carries its own protective armor in the form of eight plates on its back. This specimen lived in Clallam Bay, Washington.

SNAIL TALES

Class **Gastropoda** (which means "stomach foot") is the largest group of mollusks, with about 80,000 species. Most gastropods have a single shell, which is often coiled in a spiral. But slugs, which you may find crawling in a garden at night, do not have any shell. Most gastropods also have well-developed sense organs and creep about on a muscular foot. (Snails glide along on trails of slimy mucus secreted by their bodies. These slowpokes move only about 10 feet [3 meters] in an hour!) A gastropod has a head with eyes, tentacles for feeling and smelling, and a tonguelike radula to scrape its food off rocks.

The many ocean-dwelling gastropods include the limpets, which have conelike shells; abalones with flat spiral shells that are often used to make buttons; periwinkles,

A periwinkle (Littorina angulifera) *has a pretty shell that is often included in shell collections.*

which have pretty shells and eyes at the base of their tentacles; and sea slugs, whose shell-less bodies are often brightly colored. Sea snails breathe with gills, but freshwater snails have lungs and must come up to the surface to breathe.

Land snails have two pairs of tentacles, with eyes at the top of the rear pair, like tiny periscopes. They can pull their tentacle tips in to protect their eyes. The snails served in French restaurants (escargots) belong to the land-snail species *Helix pomatia*.

TWO SHELLS

Class **Pelecypoda** ("hatchet foot") includes about 15,000 species of mollusks whose soft bodies are protected by two shells joined by a hinge. (The class is also called Bivalvia, meaning "two shells.") This group includes clams, mussels, oysters, and scallops, all of which people eat. Bivalves are all water animals; most live in the ocean, although some are found in freshwater. They filter water through large gills, which screen out bits of food and absorb oxygen. But a bivalve has to keep its shells open to take in water, exposing part of its soft body. Powerful muscles can clamp the shells tightly shut when danger is near.

Bivalves' bodies are not as complex as those of snails. They have no head, and their sense organs are not very developed. Most spend their lives in one place, but

This scallop is the proud owner of many tiny blue eyes. The common bay scallop of North America (Argopectin irradians) is one of several species harvested for food.

many have a hatchet-shaped muscular foot that is used for burrowing in sand. Scallops are an exception. They have a row of tiny blue eyes (sometimes hundreds of them) that peep out of their shells, and they can swim, zigzagging rapidly through the water by clapping their shells together.

THE BRAINY CLASS

The members of class **Cephalopoda** ("head-foot")—cuttlefish, nautiluses, octopuses, and squids—seem very different from other mollusks. Many of the more than 600 species of cephalopods are free-swimming animals that do not have shells, and they prey on other animals. In many ways they are like vertebrate animals. Many have a support structure that resembles a skeleton. Their heads are large, with well-developed sense organs (especially eyes, which resemble vertebrate eyes) and large brains. (Their name comes from their large heads.) A cephalopod's muscular foot is usually divided into tentacles around the head.

When in danger, cephalopods squirt dark-colored chemicals into the water. Under the cover of the inky cloud that forms, the cephalopod can swim safely away. Dark ink would not be much help to the deepwater cephalopods; they cover their escapes by squirting out luminous chemicals that form a brightly glowing cloud.

Squids have eight arms and two long tentacles. The giant squid *Architeuthis* is the largest of all the invertebrates. Its tentacles can reach up to 60 feet (18 meters). It also has the largest eyes in the animal kingdom—up to 1 foot (30 centimeters) wide! A giant squid may even be able to fight off a sperm whale! Squids can move very quickly, but they swim backward. They shoot out jets of water, producing powerful jet propulsion. Some squids can even rocket out of the water and land 100 feet (30 meters) away!

Squids and cuttlefish do not have shells on the outside of their bodies, but do have some inside their bodies. They can also change color to camouflage themselves or attract mates.

Octopuses (the name of their order, **Octopoda**, means "eight feet") are the only cephalopods with no shell at all. Like squids and cuttlefish, octopuses propel themselves backward. But they use their eight long arms, equipped with two rows of suction disks on each one, to move forward. Some octopuses are less than 1.5 inches (about 3 centimeters) wide. The bodies of the largest are only about 1.5 feet (45 centimeters) wide, but their arm span may be as much as 32 feet (about 10 meters). An octopus's rubbery body is so flexible that it can squeeze into cracks in rocks and coral reefs to make its den. An octopus has a sharp beak like a parrot's that it uses to rip food apart and to break into tough shells. The suckers on an octopus's arms are very sensitive and can tell small differences in texture. These suckers also contain receptors that can taste some things better than our tongues can.

Octopus vulgaris (*vulgaris* means "common") lives in warm seas in holes along the rocky bottom. After mating, a female octopus hangs thousands of fertilized eggs from the roof of her den. For weeks she blows water over them to clean them and never leaves the den. Shortly after the eggs hatch and the tiny 0.25-inch- (6-millimeter-) long octopuses swim away, the mother dies.

An octopus can change colors like a chameleon. It turns red when it is angry or excited, white when it is frightened (this makes it look larger to a predator), and it can turn blue, green, purple, or brown to camouflage itself by matching its surroundings. Octopuses are rather intelligent. They have even been taught to "read" letterlike shapes.

The sharp beak of a common cuttlefish looks like a parrot's beak. It is used to tear up food.

Nautiluses are the only cephalopods with shells on the outside of the body. The shell is divided into chambers. The nautilus lives in the largest chamber. When it grows too big for its shell, it adds on another chamber. The empty chambers are filled with a gas that makes swimming easier. Nautiluses have about ninety arms. There are only about half a dozen species today, found in the South Pacific and Indian Oceans. One hundred million years ago there were close to 2,500 different species of nautiluses.

MOLLUSK FUN FACTS

- In ancient Greek mythology, Aphrodite (the goddess of beauty) was said to have come out of a scallop shell.
- The giant clam *Tridacna derasa* is so big that you could take a bath in one of its shells.
- If you find a clam shell, you can figure out how old it is by counting its growth lines like the rings in a tree stump—one line for every year of growth.
- A pearl is formed when a grain of sand or a small creature gets between the shell and mantle of an oyster. To protect its soft body, the oyster secretes layers of pearl around the irritant.
- An oyster can change its sex back and forth between male and female. An oyster may produce millions of eggs each year.

7

THE BIGGEST PHYLUM

If you judge by the number of species, arthropods are the animal kingdom's biggest success. There are more species of arthropods than of all the other phyla combined!

Short-horned grasshoppers belong to the family Acrididae. Swarms of these insects may destroy whole crops of grain.

More than one million species of animals have been classified in phylum **Arthropoda**, and there may really be as many as fifty million arthropod species in the world.

Arthropoda means "joint-foot." The members of this phylum have at least three pairs of tubelike legs or appendages that can bend. (An arthropod's mouthparts and sense organs are often adapted legs.) The other major characteristic of arthropods is a tough outer skeleton. Arthropods, like the annelid worms, also have segmented bodies. Many body activities are controlled at a segment level. If the brain of a grasshopper is removed, for example, it can still walk, jump, and fly.

ANNELIDS AND ARTHROPODS

Because arthropods are segmented, scientists believe they arose from the same ancestors as annelids. But during the course of evolution, the body became shorter, with fewer segments. In the annelids, each body segment is basically the same, but in arthropods the segments became more specialized. In more advanced arthropods this evolution has been taken even further—segments have become fused together to form specific body regions such as a head, **thorax**, and abdomen. (In some arthropods the head and thorax are fused into a **cephalothorax**.) However, if you look at immature forms of these arthropods (caterpillars and other larvae), the segmented body is clear.

The light **cuticle** around annelid worms became thicker and harder in arthropods and provides support for their bodies. Some annelid worms move around with paddles, but the arthropods evolved legs that are bendable and allow them to move about better. Their muscles also became more efficient. In arthropods the breathing system is much more efficient, too. They have highly developed nervous systems with complicated sense organs, including antennae and eyes.

FURTHER EVOLUTION

As arthropods evolved, they branched into three main groups: the **chelicerates** ("fanged" forms), aquatic **mandibulates** ("jawed" forms), and terrestrial mandibulates. The differences between these groups are very visible. In both the aquatic (class **Crustacea**) and terrestrial mandibulates (**Insecta** and four smaller classes), the first one or two pairs of appendages are antennae. The next pair are jaws (**mandibles**, which give this group its name). Scientists believe these two groups arose from different ancestors because the jaw structure and development are different. The other group of arthropods, the chelicerates, includes the classes **Merostomata** (horseshoe crabs), **Pycnogonida** (sea spiders), and **Arachnida** (spiders, scorpions, mites, and ticks). Chelicerates do not have antennae or mandibles. Their first pair of appendages are pincers or fangs called chelicerae.

ANIMALS IN ARMOR

An arthropod's **exoskeleton** is like a suit of armor that protects the soft tissue underneath. It is made up of three layers. The outer layer is waterproof and waxy; the middle layer is stiff; and the inner layer is made up of **chitin**, which is like the cellulose that forms the cell walls of plants. An exoskeleton is a good form of protection, both from injury and from drying out, but makes it hard to move. Fortunately the exoskeleton is in sections held together by movable joints; otherwise movement would be almost impossible. Growing also presents a problem. Arthropods have to shed their outgrown chitin coats and grow new ones many times during their lives. This is called **molting**. Many arthropods hide someplace safe while they molt because, with their protective armor gone, the animals are easier to attack.

LEGS OFFER A CLUE

If you have a collection of things—stamps or rocks or baseball cards—you already know how difficult it can be to sort them all out so that you can find the ones you want to look at and know where to put new ones. Imagine trying to classify a million species of arthropods! It's no wonder that you'll find differences in almost every reference book you check. Though scientists don't agree on all the fine details, they do agree on some basic principles. One key is that arthropods are grouped according to the number of legs they have.

Many people enjoy eating lobsters. The best lobster meat comes from lobsters that live in the North Atlantic Ocean. Lobsters belong to the class Malacostraca

Millipedes and centipedes don't really have a thousand or a hundred legs as their names suggest, but they are many-legged. Crustaceans such as barnacles, crayfish, lobsters, and shrimp have ten legs. Arachnids (spiders, scorpions, mites, and ticks) have eight legs. Insects have six legs.

FOSSILS AND LIVING FOSSILS

Trilobites were animals that lived in the ocean but are now extinct. They had many two-branched appendages, each with a leglike part and a feathery gill. Some, but not all, experts think that they were the ancestors of modern arthropods.

Onychophora is a group of "walking worms" believed to be a link between annelids and arthropods. These animals have wormlike bodies that are segmented. Their short legs (one pair for each segment) are not jointed. The feet around the mouth are used to capture and tear up prey. Taxonomists can't agree on where to put this group. Some call it a phylum, others a class under phylum Arthropoda. But all agree that it is a very old group that has changed very little over the last 500 million years.

Tardigrada is a group of more than 400 species of tiny animals that live in oceans and freshwater, in soil and forest litter, and in various other moist land habitats. Under a microscope, tardigrades look like miniature eight-legged bears, so they are often called water bears. Taxonomists usually place them in a separate phylum; its name, which means "slow step," comes from their lumbering, bearlike walk. Like onychophorans, tardigrades seem to fit in somewhere between annelids and arthropods.

Horseshoe crabs (class Merostomata) are not really crabs. Their closest living relatives are the spiders, scorpions, and other members of the class Arachnida. They are also remarkably similar to fossil forms that lived 400 to 500 million years ago. For this reason, scientists call the four living species of horseshoe crabs "living fossils."

Horseshoe crabs are found on the east coasts of Asia and North America. They do not have antennae or jaws, but they do have small pincers. Their bodies are covered by large plates. Horseshoe crabs have two large compound eyes that can see images. (Each contains about 1,000 simple eyes.) They also have several other simple eyes on various parts of their body, including the tail. (These can only make out light and dark.) Scientists have studied horseshoe-crab vision for many years because their light receptors are much bigger than those of most other animals, so they are easier to observe.

THE SPIDER KIN

Chelicerates have no antennae or jaws. They have four pairs of legs for walking, a pair of modified legs for handling food, and, in most spiders, a pair of modified appendages (**chelicerae**) that are used as poison fangs. They were originally ocean dwellers, and the horseshoe crabs and sea spiders still live in the sea. One group, the arachnids, became very successful on land. It includes spiders, daddy longlegs, scorpions, ticks, and mites.

Many chelicerates are predators. A chelicerate's body is usually divided into a cephalothorax (head and thorax are joined) and abdomen. Most members of the class Arachnida live on land and

DID YOU KNOW?

The class name Arachnida comes from ancient Greek mythology. A young girl named Arachne challenged the goddess Athena to a weaving contest. Athena was angry because Arachne's silken cloth was perfect, so she turned her into a spider.

DID YOU KNOW?

A spider's silk thread can hold 4,000 times the spider's weight! It is stronger than a steel wire of the same diameter. But commercial production of spider silk isn't practical. Scientists are working on a project to mass produce spider silk, not by spiders but by *E. coli* bacteria genetically altered to produce the silk thread.

breathe with **book lungs** consisting of thin hollow sheets of tissue like the pages of a book. They do not have compound eyes like insects, and, in fact, some have no eyes. They rely more on their sense of touch. All are carnivores, except for some types of mites. Most arachnids drink their food. When they pierce an insect with their fangs, an enzyme begins to digest the soft tissue.

More than half of the 75,000 known species of arachnids are spiders, belonging to the order **Araneae**. There are seventy families of spiders, and all of them can spin silk. (Silk is a liquid protein that hardens when exposed to air.) *Arachnida* means "web," but not all spiders use their silk to spin webs. A web-spinning spider doesn't have to learn to spin a web; as soon as it hatches, it knows how. There are about 15,000 kinds of spiders that spin webs. Each kind spins its own unique kind of web.

Some spiders live underground and come out to hunt for insects. Trap-door spiders use silk to line their tube-shaped burrow and the underside of a trapdoor that covers the entrance. If an insect walks over the door, the spider jumps out, grabs its victim, and pulls it down into the tube. Some spiders, such as *Argyroneta aquatica* (which is found in Europe and Asia), live underwater. This spider builds an underwater web and brings air bubbles down to the web to breathe.

Most spiders have eight eyes on top of their heads but have poor eyesight. Their sense of touch is very acute, though. The spider's entire body, including mouthparts and legs, is covered with sensory hairs that can detect the slightest movement. The mouthparts are called pedipalps. They squeeze out body juices from the spider's prey.

All spiders are poisonous, but very few are dangerous to humans because the amount of venom the spider injects is very small. Even a bite from a female black widow spider, *Latrodectus mactans*, rarely kills human victims. A female black widow is much bigger than the male. A male has to be very careful when trying to mate—the female might eat him instead.

The hairy, long-legged tarantulas of South American jungles are the largest spiders—they are up to 10 inches (25 centimeters) wide with their legs stretched out! That's the size of a dinner plate!

When spiders are young, they may go ballooning. They wait on the edge of a blade

The spider Arabella successfully spun a web in the zero gravity of space.

of grass or a plant, and when a breeze comes along, they spin out long silk strands. The spiders float away on the wind and can travel great distances. Some have been found floating 2,000 feet (610 meters) up in the air, or 200 miles (322 kilometers) out to sea.

The daddy longlegs or harvestmen of the order **Opiliones** look like spiders, but they aren't because they don't have silk glands. Daddy longlegs die shortly after they mate in the fall, but their eggs hatch in the spring to start the next generation. They are called harvestmen because they are most visible at harvesttime.

The arachnids also include several orders of scorpions, pseudoscorpions, and whip scorpions. The 700 species in the order **Scorpionida** live in tropics and deserts around the world. They vary in size from 0.5 inch to 8 inches (1.3 to 20 centimeters). Scorpions have eight eyes on their backs. During the day they hide from the heat of the sun, but at night they come out and hunt insects. A scorpion has a long slender tail that is held up over its back when it walks. It stings with its tail. The venom of most scorpions is not dangerous to humans, although a sting can be painful. However, scorpions of the genus *Centruroides sculpturatus* in the Southwest have extremely toxic venom that can be fatal to humans.

There are about 20,000 species of mites and ticks, belonging to the order **Acari**. Many live on the bodies of large animals and plants, and some cause diseases. Others hunt tiny roundworms in the soil or eat insect eggs.

SHELLFISH IN ARMOR

Crustacea means "with a crust or shell." This group is named for the tough chitin shield, or carapace, that covers the animal's head and back. (Like the arachnids, a crustacean's head and thorax are usually joined into a single unit.) The more than 45,000 species range from tiny water fleas and copepods, just a fraction of a millimeter long, to the lobsters and crabs that people like to eat. Most crustaceans live in the water (they are found in all the oceans of the world, as well as in freshwater lakes and streams), but a few, such as pill bugs, live on land. Insects don't live in salt water, and crustaceans fill the place in the sea that insects take up in the rest of the world. Most crustaceans have a larval stage that swims around before developing into the adult form. The water-dwelling crustaceans have gills for breathing.

Crustaceans can live in environments where few other animals can survive. Krill, which are small shrimplike animals, live in the icy Antarctic Ocean. The very salty Great Salt Lake in Utah is home to few animals, but brine shrimp live there.

All crustaceans have ten legs, and most have two pairs of antennae. Their appendages are two-branched. Some crustaceans have eyes on movable stalks.

THE LOBSTER CLAN

There are about 8,000 species in the order **Decapoda**, which includes the most familiar crustaceans, such as lobsters, crabs, shrimp, and crayfish. The first pair of legs are much larger, with thick pincer claws. Decapods are flat either on the sides (lobsters) or on the top and bottom (crabs).

If you've ever eaten lobster, it was probably a Maine lobster, *Homarus americanus*. A lobster has a typical crustacean body plan. Its front two legs are giant pincers that are shaped differently from each other. One is designed to hold its prey and the other to crush it. The lobster's stomach has teeth that break down food. Blood is pumped into body spaces by a heart. One pair of antennae is used for seeing and the other pair for feeling. The nervous system consists of a brain and a long nerve cord. When eggs are fertilized, they are carried in a special pouch. When they become larvae, they swim away to begin life on their own.

A crayfish looks like a little lobster. In addition to the two eyes on a crayfish's head, there is an eye on its tail!

Shrimp swim backward! Red shrimp have been found nearly 7 miles (11 kilometers) deep in the ocean. Some types of shrimp are males when they are young, but then turn into females when they are big enough to carry eggs.

Crabs' body proportions are quite different from those of lobsters. In crabs the abdomen is tucked under the body, and the cephalothorax is larger and broader than the abdomen. Some crabs live both in water and on land, and some are completely terrestrial. Crabs walk and run sideways. There are about 4,500 different kinds of crabs.

A female fiddler crab's two front claws are the same size, but one of the male's claws is much larger than the other. The male waves the huge claw to attract a female and to warn other males away. The waving motion reminded people of a fiddler playing a fiddle.

Hermit crabs don't have shells of their own, so they live inside empty snail shells. When the hermit crab is too big for the shell, it finds another. Some hermit crabs may place sea anemones on top of their shells for protection. When the hermit crab moves into a new shell, the sea anemone moves with it. The robber crab, *Birgus latro*, of the South Pacific climbs palm trees to get coconuts to eat. It is the largest of the land crabs—a hermit crab that is too big to find empty shells to live in.

This hermit crab has made a home out of an empty shell.

OTHER NOTABLE CRUSTACEANS

Copepods are the smallest of the crustaceans; most are only 0.02 to 0.4 inch (0.5 to 10 millimeters) long. Yet there are so many copepods in the surface waters of the oceans that they are one of the most important food sources for fish. There are more individual copepods than any other animal. Scientists estimate that the number in the copepod genus *Calanus* is greater than the number of all other animals combined!

Barnacles look like mollusks, and early taxonomists placed them in phylum Mollusca. But when scientists learned more about a barnacle's life cycle, they changed their minds—the larvae are like arthropod larvae. A barnacle larva attaches its head to a rock or boat hull, and then its body changes. Its eyes dissolve and it secretes limy plates around itself and no longer moves around. An adult barnacle looks something like a volcano. It sticks its legs out to catch food.

Barnacles are saltwater shellfish that attach themselves to almost anything underwater. People in the marine industry are trying to develop products that will prevent barnacles from attaching themselves to boats and wharves.

MANY-LEGGERS

Centipedes and millipedes look like worms at first glance, but they are arthropods because they have exoskeletons and jointed legs. Their internal organs are also much more complicated. These two groups of arthropods were once grouped together, but scientists now know they are not closely related.

Centipedes have from 15 to 173 segments, with a pair of legs for each body segment. Even their long antennae contain at least 12 segments. These arthropods are carnivores that hunt various small animals. A poison produced by their claws can paralyze their victims—insects, earthworms, or even lizards! About 3,000 species of centipedes have been described. The most common is the house centipede, *Scutigera forceps*, which you might find in your house. It is about 2 inches (5 centimeters) long and has fifteen pairs of legs. A species found in the West Indies, *Scolopendra gigas*, is the largest centipede. It grows to 12 inches (30 centimeters) long and sometimes catches mice and lizards.

Millipedes have two pairs of legs for each body segment. (Actually, each body segment is really two segments fused together.) Most have about thirty-five segments, but the number can range from twenty-five to one hundred. Their legs move in a wave-like rhythm. Millipedes' antennae are shorter than those of centipedes, and they do not have poisonous claws. They don't need such aggressive weapons because they eat decaying vegetation. When danger threatens, a millipede curls up in a tight coil so that its soft underside is protected. Millipedes can also give off a foul-smelling liquid to keep attackers away. About 7,500 species have been classified. They range in length from 0.06 inch to 12 inches (1.6 to 300 millimeters). *Spirobolus marginatus* is a reddish brown or black millipede, common in the eastern United States. It is 4 inches (10 centimeters) long and about as thick as a pencil. *Luminodesmus sequoiae*, a species found in California, can light up in the dark.

All this huge diversity would be enough to make the arthropods one of the animal kingdom's biggest success stories. But you haven't even met the real stars of the arthropod show: the class Insecta. You'll find out about them in the next chapter.

8

EARTH'S RULING CLASS

If you were that alien explorer we talked about in the first two chapters, after studying the many animals you encountered, you might try to communicate with . . . an insect!

Insects are the most successful group of living creatures that have ever lived on our planet. They make up the largest class of living things. Three-quarters of all the species in the animal kingdom belong to this class, and each species has huge numbers of members. Scientists estimate that at any one time there are a quadrillion insects on the earth. They can be found in almost every habitat, except in salt water. There is even a species of fly that spends part of its life in crude petroleum.

WHAT IS AN INSECT?

Insects are a class in phylum Arthropoda. All adult insects have three pairs of legs and a body that is divided into three parts: the head, the thorax, and the abdomen. The heads of most insects have a pair of antennae, complicated eyes, and large jaws. (Insects may use their antennae to taste, feel, or smell.)

Many insects have wings; they are the only invertebrates that fly. Most flying insects have two pairs of wings, one for flying and one for balancing. Some, such as flies and mosquitoes, have only one pair and some, such as fleas, have no wings. Still others, such as ants and termites, are normally wingless but periodically produce special winged forms for mating or migration to another place.

Scientists who study insects are called **entomologists**. These scientists divide insects into twenty-five to thirty different orders. Nearly all of the insects that you've heard of, however, belong to fewer than a dozen orders. One of the main characteristics used to classify insects is the type of wing.

INSECT EVOLUTION

Scientists believe that insects evolved from a centipede-like ancestor. The first insects were like their ancestors but had only three pairs of legs. The next major development was the evolution of wings. Dragonflies and mayflies are believed to belong to the most primitive orders of winged insects because, unlike all the others, their wings cannot be folded over their backs when at rest.

The ancestors of today's dragonfly lived millions of years ago. A dragonfly has keen eyesight and has been known to fly 50 to 60 miles (80 to 97 kilometers) an hour.

AMAZING METAMORPHOSIS

A human baby looks different from an adult, but the differences are mostly in size. Both have the same basic body parts. But most insect babies don't just grow larger; they develop in several very different stages—as though a chick turned into a dog that grew some more and then became a human adult. This process of developing through major changes is called **metamorphosis**, which means "change in form."

Butterflies lay eggs that hatch into caterpillars (larvae). The larvae don't look at all like butterflies. They have long, segmented, wormlike bodies with many legs and no wings. Their mouths and body parts look very different, too. The caterpillar eats and eats and sheds its skin each time it gets too tight. When the caterpillar gets to the right size, it buries itself in the ground or attaches itself to a leaf, and its outer covering hardens into a tough, protective case. It has turned into a **pupa**. Inside the case, dramatic changes are occurring. The caterpillar's body actually melts into a liquid, and new body parts form. Finally, a butterfly with long, jointed legs and antennae, compound eyes, and brightly colored wings breaks out of the case. It looks nothing like either the pupa or the larva.

Many insects—including moths, butterflies, bees, beetles, and flies—undergo complete metamorphosis. But other insects do not go through all of these stages.

YUM OR YUCK?

In many areas of the world, people eat insects such as ants, beetles, caterpillars, grasshoppers, grubs, locusts, and termites. They are great sources of protein!

A cicada has just undergone its final molt and has its adult wings. It sits atop its shed skin.

Some insects, such as grasshoppers and dragonflies, hatch out as nymphs, which look like tiny copies of their parents except that they have no wings. Each time they shed their skin, they look more like their parents, and after the final molt they have their adult wings. This kind of gradual change is called incomplete metamorphosis. Insects from evolutionary older orders molt more times than more advanced insects. Mayflies molt thirty or more times, but locusts only four or five times.

CONTROLLING INSECTS

Less than 1 percent of all insects are major pests. But the damage done by this 1 percent can be great, and the amount of money spent each year to control them adds up to billions of dollars. Using chemical pesticides is one method of control. Importing insects, such as ladybugs, that prey on damaging insects is another. Tiny wasps and other parasites that lay their eggs in the bodies of insects or their larvae can be effective, too. *Bacillus thuringiensis*, a bacterium that causes a fatal disease in moths and other insect pests, is sold in the form of a powder that can be used as a natural pesticide. An even more imaginative approach is the use of traps scented with sex pheromones, the odor chemicals that female insects use to attract mates.

ORDER ODONATA ("TOOTH")

The dragonfly is one of the oldest insects, and the first animal to fly. Dragonflies and damselflies have large eyes and long, slender abdomens with two pairs of large wings. Although they don't have teeth, they are fierce hunters. A type of dragonfly with a four-foot wingspan lived millions of years ago. This is the largest insect that ever lived on earth. *Megaloprepus caerulatus* of Central and South America, with a wingspan of about 7 inches (18 centimeters), is the largest dragonfly alive today. Dragonflies live about two years in the water as nymphs. Then they live for less than two weeks as adults.

ORDER COLEOPTERA ("SHEATH WINGS")

The largest group of insects includes 300,000 known species of beetles, weevils, and fireflies. These insects have a horny sheath covering their second pair of wings.

If you go bug watching in the northeastern United States, you're likely to see plenty of Japanese beetles. It is believed that these pests first arrived here in 1916 when beetle larvae made the journey in potted plants imported to New Jersey from Japan.

Not all imported insects are unwanted pests, though. Ladybugs were imported from Australia to southern California in 1892 to help eliminate insects that were damaging citrus crops. Farmers in Australia had a problem when 6 million acres (2.4 million hectares) of land were ruined because of the dung created by their cattle. Dung beetles were imported to break down the dung and help make the land usable again.

*This monster beetle (*Goliathus*) lives in the Ituri rain forest in Zaire.*

The Goliath beetle is the heaviest insect in the world. This 4-inch- (10-centimeter-) long beetle can weigh almost 0.25 pound (0.11 kilogram)! Children in Africa sometimes tie strings around these beetles, which then fly in circles around the children's heads, whirring like airplanes as they go.

SUPERORDER ORTHOPTERODEA ("STRAIGHT WINGS")

Several orders of insects all have straight wings and are now grouped by some taxonomists into a large superorder. Grasshoppers, locusts, crickets, and katydids all chew plants and make up the order **Orthoptera**.

Grasshoppers and crickets are among the few insects that can hear. They have eardrums on their legs or the sides of their abdomens. Only male crickets chirp. In some Asian countries crickets are kept for pets because their owners enjoy their chirping. Actually, insects don't have voices. Their songs are made by rubbing one body part against another. Grasshoppers, for example, rub their front wings against knobs on the insides of their hind legs.

Praying mantises (now placed in the order **Mantodea**) are carnivores that hunt their prey. Their name comes from the way they hold their front legs while lying in wait. They also seem to wash their faces the same way house cats do. Some species of mantids are so big that they eat birds, frogs, and lizards!

Walking sticks (order **Phasmida** or Phasmatoptera) are the longest living insects, growing up to 13 inches long (a third of a meter). They look amazingly like the woody stems of shrubs; other phasmids are near-perfect copies of leaves, complete with vein patterns and fake disease spots. Their protective camouflage works because they spend much of the time standing still on branches.

Many people have found out the hard way that cockroaches (order **Blattodea**) are difficult to get rid of. These insects have remained practically unchanged for 250 million years because they can endure a wide range of conditions. They can eat almost anything, including glue, paint, even fingernail clippings and human hair. They can be frozen, and when they thaw out, they are fine. They can withstand one hundred times more radiation than a human can. Even if it loses its head, a cockroach will live for several weeks before it finally starves to death. Some scientists find cockroaches useful. They are used in cancer research because they develop cancerous tumors similar to some of those found in humans.

ORDER HEMIPTERA ("HALF WINGS")

People call all kinds of creatures bugs (even bacteria and viruses), but scientists call only one order of insects "true bugs." These include bedbugs, chinch bugs, squash bugs, and water boatmen. A bug's wings are folded over its body when it isn't using them to fly. Bugs have mouths that pierce and suck. Bedbugs suck human blood. The chinch bug and squash bug damage crops. Bugs do not go through a pupal stage during their metamorphosis.

HOMOPTERA ("SIMILAR WINGS")

Aphids and cicadas have sucking mouthparts and can damage crops. People call cicadas "seventeen-year locusts," but locusts are very different. Locusts look like large grasshoppers and move in groups of millions. Cicadas look like hornets and are the ones that make the familiar shrill sound heard on summer nights. The cicada *Magicicada septendecem* lives as a nymph sucking sap from the roots of a tree. Then, after seventeen years, the nymphs climb up the tree, molt, and become adults.

ORDER DIPTERA ("TWO WINGS")

Flies, gnats, and mosquitoes have only a single pair of wings. (However, they also have a pair of knobbed organs for balancing.) Flies eat only liquid foods like blood, sweat, honey, and nectar. Dipterans are major pests for humans. Some carry diseases. Some mosquitoes spread malaria and yellow fever; houseflies spread germs.

A housefly lives for only two to three weeks. Flyswatters are designed with holes in them because flies are very sensitive to changes in air pressure. The holes in the flyswatter reduce the change in air pressure of an approaching swat.

Only female mosquitoes bite people; the males feed on plant juices, pollen, and nectar. As carriers of malaria, mosquitoes have caused more human deaths than all the

---

AMAZING INSECT FACTS

Insects are very strong. If you were as strong as a beetle, you would be able to lift 10,000 pounds (4,530 kilograms)!

Millions of monarch butterflies stop each year in the town of Pacific Grove, California, during their yearly migration from Canada and Alaska down to Mexico and Central America.

Humans have 792 muscles; caterpillars have 4,000!

A male gypsy moth can pick up the scent of a female 7 miles (11 kilometers) away.

It takes up to 2,500 silkworm cocoons to make 1 pound (0.45 kilogram) of silk.

The deer botfly is the fastest flying insect, reaching a speed of 36 miles per hour (58 kilometers per hour).

Bumblebees beat their wings 130 times a second. Honeybee wings beat almost twice as fast.

The bees in a single hive can produce up to 2 pounds (about 1 kilogram) of honey each day. That takes five million trips to gather pollen and nectar!

wars in history. The common gnat, *Culex pipiens*, is really a mosquito. In fact, *gnat* is the Old English word for mosquito.

ORDER LEPIDOPTERA ("SCALE WINGS")

A large cluster of Monarch butterflies (Danaus plexippus) *rest on a eucalyptus tree in California. The tops of their wings are brightly colored. When the wings are folded, the underside shows and appears as a light gray.*

People often find it difficult to tell the difference between a butterfly and a moth. Both have stiff wings that are covered with overlapping scales. (This is what gives the wings their color, and this order its name.) On butterfly wings the scales are flat, but on moths they are almost hairlike. Butterfly wings are often more brightly colored. Butterflies have knobs at the tips of their antennae; most moths have feathery feelers. When they are resting, a moth spreads its wings flat, but a butterfly folds its wings over its back. One of the easiest ways to tell them apart, though, is *when* you see them. Butterflies fly in the daytime, and moths fly at night. The caterpillars of many moths and butterflies damage crops. The cocoon of the silkworm moth, *Bombyx mori* (which is its pupal stage), is used to make silk. Silkworm moths can't fly because this species has been domesticated by people for so long. There are about 150,000 species of lepidopterans—this is about 15 percent of all insects!

ORDER ISOPTERA ("EQUAL WINGS")

Termites eat wood and spend their time tunneling through houses and fallen trees. Many termites cannot digest wood without help from tiny protozoa that live in their digestive tract. They break down the wood fibers so the termites can digest their food.

Trinervitermes, an African genus of termites, builds nests that may be 130 feet (40 meters) deep. Spanish settlers in Brazil used one type of termite nest as ovens, because the clay material the termites used was so hard.

Termites are **social insects**. They live in complex communities where each member has a specific place. Small worker termites do all the necessary jobs and care for the huge queen, who does nothing but lay eggs. The queen of one tropical termite species can live up to fifty years!

ORDER HYMENOPTERA ("MEMBRANE WINGS")

Ants, bees, and wasps are also social insects. Among bumblebees and honeybees, drones (fertile males) hatch out of eggs that were not fertilized. The workers are females that cannot reproduce. Only the queen can produce new bees. Worker ants are also females that cannot reproduce. Once a year, fertile winged males and females hatch and fly out of the anthill to mate and set up new colonies.

Most of the 200,000 species in this order have a characteristic narrowing between the thorax and abdomen. (You can easily tell a termite from an ant because the termite has a thick "waist.")

OTHER NOTABLE INSECTS

Lice (order **Anoplura**) are wingless insects that are parasites on humans and other animals. They glue their eggs (called nits) to their host's hair. Sometimes schools have to be closed because of an outbreak of head lice, which are easily spread among children.

Fleas (order **Siphonaptera**) are bloodsucking parasites on people and animals. The Black Death, the devastating plague that swept through Europe in the Middle Ages, was a bacterial disease spread by fleas on rats that got into people's houses. Plague germs still exist but rarely kill people anymore; the disease is kept in check by better sanitation.

Fleas escape from their enemies by jumping. In proportion to their body size, they are the champion jumpers of the animal world. A flea can jump 7 inches (18 centimeters) into the air or broad-jump 13 inches (33 centimeters)—300 times its own length. Jumps are powered by a rubberlike protein.

9

THE SPINY-SKINNED

Starfish and sea urchins are members of the phylum **Echinodermata**. There are about 7,000 species of echinoderms, including brittle stars, feather stars, sand dollars, sea cucumbers, and sea lilies, all of which live in the sea. *Echinoderm* means "spiny-skinned"; most of these animals have a type of internal skeleton made of limy plates under the skin, with spiny projections sticking out. The echinoderm circulatory system is unique in the animal kingdom. Seawater is used as a circulatory fluid. The vascular system consists of water-filled canals that end in thousands of tiny tube feet. These feet

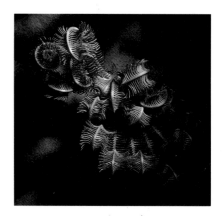

A sea lily growing in the Red Sea

may be used for moving, feeding, or respiration. At first it may seem strange that this phylum is placed closer to the vertebrates than all of the other phyla we've discussed. Starfish are interesting, but they don't seem as advanced as other invertebrates. Most are radially symmetrical (in a five-fold pattern), not bilateral like most vertebrates. They don't have heads or brains, and their nervous systems are not centralized. They don't even have excretory organs. However, the larvae (young forms) are usually bilaterally symmetrical, and when scientists observe the embryonic stages of the echinoderms, they find remarkable similarities to the vertebrates.

ROUNDABOUT HISTORY

Biologists believe that echinoderms have gone through three stages of evolution. Early echinoderms were bilaterally symmetrical and free-swimming. But they evolved into radially symmetric creatures like the sea lilies, which did not move about because staying in one place was more advantageous for filter feeding (filtering out small particles of food from the water). In the third evolutionary stage, free-moving starfish and sea urchins evolved.

CLASS ASTEROIDEA: STARS OF THE SEA

Starfish (sometimes called sea stars) are star-shaped, usually with five arms. (Some have six arms and some have up to twenty-five or fifty arms.) They come in many colors, such as green, purple, red, yellow, or black. They have rows of tube feet on the undersides of their arms. A starfish walks on its arm tips, using the sucker action of the tube feet to cling to a surface. It can also swim by waving its arms up and down.

Starfish eat the soft bodies inside the hard shells of clams and oysters. They wrap their arms around clamshells, using their tube feet like suction cups to hold on tight, and pry them open. Starfish have a strange way of eating. Most animals bring food into their mouths and swallow it down into their stomachs. But the starfish turns its stomach inside out and pushes it out of its mouth (which is on the underside of its body), in through the opening between the shells of its bivalve prey, and digests the clam's soft body right inside its shells. When the food is all digested, the starfish pulls its stomach back inside its body.

This colorful starfish, Northern Sea Star (Asterias vulgaris), *was photographed near Rockport, Massachusetts, as it walked along on the tips of its arms.*

DID YOU KNOW?

Oyster fishers have always hated starfish because these echinoderms can destroy a whole bed of clams or oysters in a single night. When they pulled up starfish from the water, the oystermen would tear them apart and throw them back into the water, thinking they were killing these seafood competitors. They didn't know that if a starfish loses an arm, it will grow a new one. In fact, the lost arm itself may grow into a whole new starfish!

Brittle stars, basket stars, and serpent stars look like starfish but have some key differences. Their five arms are longer, thinner, and branched into many smaller arms. Tube feet are not used for moving. Instead they thrash their arms around to move. Their digestive system is also very different. They have no intestine or anus, and do not push their stomachs out of their bodies. Some of the species that live in deep water can glow in the dark.

CLASS ECHINOIDEA: LIVING PINCUSHIONS

Sea urchins and sand dollars are wheel-shaped like starfish, but they do not have protruding arms. The five-part body plan is still visible, however, in the five paired rows of tube feet that push out through openings in the limy skeleton. Their bodies are covered with thousands of limy plates that are packed together, almost forming a sphere. Sea urchins look like pincushions because long spines stick out. They move around by waving these spines and moving their tube feet. Urchins dig holes in the sandy ocean bottom or even in rocks to protect themselves from pounding waves.

Red sea urchins (Strongylocentrotus francis) *display their numerous spines next to a test, which is the limy skeleton of a dead sea urchin.*

Sand dollars are almost as flat as pancakes and are covered with very short spines. They burrow in the sand to protect themselves from predators such as flounder. The limy skeletons (called "tests") of dead sand dollars may be seen on a sandy beach.

DID YOU KNOW?

Some sea urchins, such as the long-spined black sea urchin, have poisonous tips on some of their spines. The triggerfish has found a way to get around this hazard. It shoots water at the sea urchin to flip it over, because there aren't many spines on the sea urchin's underside.

CLASS HOLOTHUROIDEA: SEA CUCUMBERS

Sea cucumbers are slow-moving, tough-skinned animals that look like cucumbers. Unlike most echinoderms, they have very few limy plates under their skin and no spines. Their body plan has partly returned to a bilateral symmetry; however, they also have five rows of tube feet on the body surface. Up to thirty tentacles around the sea cucumber's mouth are used to capture food.

When threatened, some sea cucumbers shoot out bad-tasting, sticky threads from their anus, entangling the predator. Some species go even further, squirting out part or all of their digestive system and some other body organs! (They regrow the lost parts.)

CLASS CRINOIDEA: ANOTHER GROUP OF "PLANT-ANIMALS"

The most primitive living echinoderms grow on stalks that are attached to the ocean bottom. Their bodies are cup-shaped, with the mouth at the top. Around the mouth are armlike feathery rays that reach up in multiples of five. The crinoids include several types of sea lilies and feather stars, which look like feather dusters.

Although some species of sea lilies never move once they have settled down, others can use their well-developed arm muscles to crawl and swim. Sea lilies in the tropics have a strange way of moving to another place if there isn't much food: the head breaks off the stalk and walks on its arms to a better location. There it grows a new stalk.

NEW DISCOVERIES ARE WAITING

Classification is not a "dead" science. Taxonomists are constantly fitting newly discovered species into their schemes of life. In 1986, for example, the first sea daisy was reported, living in crevices of rotting wood in New Zealand waters. Not only was it a completely new echinoderm species, but it didn't fit into any of the known classes. So a new class, **Concentricycloidea**, had to be added. Later a Caribbean sea daisy species was found.

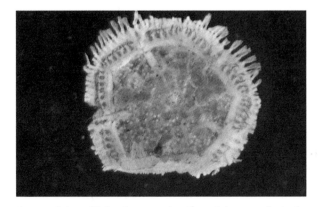

A sea daisy (Xyloplax medusiformis)—a relatively new species in the ever-evolving science of classification

IDENTIKEY

Naturalists may use identification keys to help them in identifying plants and animals. For example, suppose you were weeding the garden and found a "worm" in the soil. Here's an "identikey" to help you determine whether it is a worm, and if so, what kind.

1.	Less than 0.4 inch (1 centimeter) long, threadlike	**Roundworm**
	More than 0.4 inch (1 centimeter) long, thicker body	**Go to step 2**
2.	Soft body, moist skin	**Go to step 3**
	Tough protective outer covering over body	**Go to step 4**
3.	Body not segmented, head with antennae and eyes	**Garden slug**
	Body segmented, smooth collar, head not distinct	**Earthworm**
4.	Body segmented, thin legs on most segments	**Go to step 5**
	Segmented, short legs on front and middle segments	**A "cutworm" (moth larva)**
5.	One pair of legs on each segment	**Centipede**
	Two pairs of legs on segments, curls up when scared	**Millipede**

A LITTLE LATIN HELPS

Knowing some basic Latin and Greek "building blocks" can help you guess the meaning of scientific terms.

a-	without	*-form(es)*	in the form of,	*ov(o)-*	egg
amphi-	both		resembling	*-ped, -pod*	foot, leg
antho-	flower	*gam-*	joined; pertaining to	*-phil*	loving
aqua-	water		mating	*-phor(e)*	carrier
arthr(o)-	joint(ed)	*gen-*	gene, hereditary	*poly-*	many
bi-	two	*herb(i)-*	plant	*por-*	pore
carn(i)-	meat	*hetero-*	different	*pro-*	before
cephal(o)-	head	*hexa-*	six	*prot(o)-*	first
-coel	cavity	*homo-*	same	*-ptera*	wings
deca-	ten	*hydr-*	water	*-som(e)*	body
derm-	skin	*in-*	in, not	*-sperm*	seed
di-	two	*maxi-*	big	*stom-*	opening
endo-	inside	*mini-*	little	*terr(a)-*	land
entomo-	insect	*mon(o)-*	one	*vir-*	poison
epi-	upon, outer, besides	*-morph*	form	*-vore*	eating
eu-	true	*oct(a)-*	eight	*vulgaris*	common
exo-	outside	*-oid*	like	*-zo(o)-*	animal
fil-	thread	*oo-*	egg		

GLOSSARY

Acari — the arachnid order including mites and ticks.

Annelida — the invertebrate phylum of segmented worms, including earthworms, polychaetes, and leeches.

Anoplura — the insect order of lice.

antenna — "feelers"; appendages on the head, used as sensory organs.

Anthozoa — the class of cnidarians containing sea anemones and corals.

Arachnida — a class of arthropods including spiders, scorpions, mites, and ticks.

Araneae — the arachnid order of spiders.

Arthropoda — the invertebrate phylum including horseshoe crabs, ticks, mites, scorpions, spiders, water fleas, copepods, barnacles, lobsters, shrimp, millipedes, centipedes, and insects.

bilateral symmetry — a body form with two distinct halves, each of which is an approximate mirror image of the other.

binomial nomenclature — the system of scientific naming devised by Carl Linnaeus in which each organism is assigned a genus and a species name.

Blattodea — the insect order of cockroaches.

book lungs — the breathing organs of arachnids.

Cephalopoda — a class of mollusks includings cuttlefish, nautiluses, octopuses, and squids.

cephalothorax — a fused body structure containing the head and thorax.

Cestoda — a class of parasitic flatworms including tapeworms.

chelicerae — pincers or fangs of a spider or scorpion.

chelicerates — "fanged" forms of arthropods, such as spiders and scorpions.

chitin — a polymer containing sugar units, which forms the inner layer of an arthropod's exoskeleton.

class — a category in the classification of living organisms (the next smaller after phylum).

classification — the process of dividing objects into related groups.

Cnidaria — the invertebrate phylum including hydra, corals, sea anemones, and jellyfish.

cnidoblasts — specialized stinging cells of cnidarians.

coelom — an internal body cavity, lined with musclelike cells.

Coleoptera — the insect order of beetles.

colony — a group of cells or organisms that live in a stable association.

compound eyes — eyes consisting of many smaller units (simple eyes).

Crinoidea — a class of echinoderm that includes the sea daisy.

Crustacea — a class of aquatic arthropods including lobsters, crabs, shrimp, and crayfish.

Ctenophora — the invertebrate phylum of comb jellies.

cuticle — an outer protective covering.

Decapoda — the arachnid order including lobsters, crabs, shrimp, and crayfish.

Diptera — an insect order including flies, gnats, and mosquitoes.

Echinodermata — the invertebrate phylum including sea stars, sand dollars, sea urchins, and sea cucumbers.

eggs — female reproductive cells.

entomologist — a scientist who studies insects.

exoskeleton — a skeleton that forms an animal's outer covering.

family — a category in the classification of living organisms (the next smaller after order).

Gastropoda — a class of mollusks including snails, slugs, and limpets.

gastrovascular cavity — in cnidarians, a baglike body cavity in which digestion of food, elimination of wastes, and circulation of body fluids take place.

genus — a group of rather closely related organisms.

Hemiptera — the insect order of true bugs.

Hirudinea — a class of annelids including leeches.

Homoptera — an insect order including aphids and cicadas.

Hydrozoa — the class of cnidarians containing hydras and Portuguese man-of-war.

Hymenoptera — an insect order including ants, bees, and wasps.

Insecta — a class of arthropods consisting of insects.

invertebrate — an animal without a backbone.

Isoptera — the insect order of termites.

kingdom — the largest group in the classification of living organisms.

larva — an immature form of an animal, which usually looks quite different from the adults of its species.

Lepidoptera — an insect order including butterflies and moths.

mandibles — jaws.

mandibulates — "jawed" forms of arthropods, such as insects and crustaceans.

mantle — the covering of tissues over the internal organs of mollusks.

Mantodea — an order of carnivorous insects that includes praying mantises.

medusa — an umbrella-shaped form of a cnidarian, with the body opening at the bottom.

Merostomata — a class of arthropods including horseshoe crabs.

metamorphosis — a series of major changes in form during an animal's development.

Mollusca — the invertebrate phylum of mollusks, including monoplacophores, chitons, snails, slugs, clams, oysters, nautilus, octopus, and squid.

molting — shedding the outer covering of the body.

Monoplacophora — a class of primitive mollusks.

Nematoda — the invertebrate phylum of roundworms.

Nemertea — the invertebrate phylum of ribbon worms.

Odonata — the insect order of dragonflies.

Oligochaeta — a class of annelids including earthworms.

Onychophora — "walking worms"; a class of arthropods.

Opiliones — an arachnid order that includes the daddy longlegs.

order — a category in the classification of living organisms (the next smaller after class).

Orthoptera — the insect order including grasshoppers, crickets, locusts, and katydids.

Parazoa — in some classification systems, a subkingdom consisting of sponges.

pedipalps — mouthparts of a spider.

Pelecypoda — a class of mollusks including clams, mussels, oysters, and scallops; also called bivalves.

Phasmida — the insect order of walking sticks.

phylum — a major category in the classification of living organisms.

Platyhelminthes — the invertebrate phylum of flatworms.

Polychaeta — a class of annelids including bristle worms.

polyp — a vase-shaped form of a cnidarian, with the body opening at the top, surrounded by tentacles.

Polyplacophora — a class of mollusks including tritons.

Porifera — the invertebrate phylum of sponges.

protist — a single-celled organism; a member of kingdom Protista, in which some taxonomists also include multicellular algae.

pupa — a resting stage in an insect's life cycle, during which major reorganization of internal organs occurs within a protective outer case.

Pycnogonida — a class of arthropods including sea spiders.

radial symmetry — circular symmetry around a central point, with no distinct right and left sides.

radula — a tonguelike organ of some mollusks, used to rasp off bits of food.

Scorpionida — an arachnid order of scorpions.

Scyphozoa — the class of cnidarians containing jellyfish.

Siphonaptera — the insect order of fleas.

skeleton — a supporting framework; most invertebrates have an external skeleton.

social insects — insects that live together in complex communities, the members of which have specific tasks; bees, wasps, ants, and termites.

species — a group of very closely related organisms, each able to breed with others in the group.

sperm — male reproductive cells.

spicules — the small, hard structural units that make up the skeleton of some sponges.

Tardigrada — the invertebrate phylum of water bears.

taxonomy — the science of classifying or arranging living things into groups based on the characteristics they share.

thorax — the middle segment of an arthropod's body.

Trematoda — a class of parasitic flatworms including flukes.

tube worms — worms that live inside tubes or tunnels that they have made in the ocean bottom.

Turbellaria — the class of free-living flatworms.

vertebrate — an animal with a backbone.

INDEX

~~~~~~~